MW01602311

BREAD MACHINE COOKBOOK FOR
BEGINNERS

Quick, Easy and Delicious Recipes to Baking Homemade Bread

TRACY GORDON

© **Copyright 2020 by Tracy Gordon**
All rights reserved.

This document is geared towards providing exact and reliable information with regards to the topic and issue covered. The publication is sold with the idea that the publisher is not required to render accounting, officially permitted, or otherwise, qualified services. If advice is necessary, legal or professional, a practiced individual in the profession should be ordered.

- From a Declaration of Principles which was accepted and approved equally by a Committee of the American Bar Association and a Committee of Publishers and Associations.

In no way is it legal to reproduce, duplicate, or transmit any part of this document in either electronic means or in printed format. Recording of this publication is strictly prohibited and any storage of this document is not allowed unless with written permission from the publisher. All rights reserved.

The information provided herein is stated to be truthful and consistent, in that any liability, in terms of inattention or otherwise, by any usage or abuse of any policies, processes, or directions contained within is the solitary and utter responsibility of the recipient reader. Under no circumstances will any legal responsibility or blame be held against the publisher for any reparation, damages, or monetary loss due to the information herein, either directly or indirectly.

Respective authors own all copyrights not held by the publisher.

The information herein is offered for informational purposes solely, and is universal as so. The presentation of the information is without contract or any type of guarantee assurance.

The trademarks that are used are without any consent, and the publication of the trademark is without permission or backing by the trademark owner. All trademarks and brands within this book are for clarifying purposes only and are the owned by the owners themselves, not affiliated with this document.

TABLE OF CONTENT

CHAPTER 1: INTRODUCTION

Technology should make our lives simpler, and bread machines open a variety of choices to how we bake and eat bread. It doesn't take several ingredients to make this all possible, only 4 - flour, water, salt, and yeast. Different ingredients can be utilized for a variety of results; however, these 4 are the minimum essentials. To begin with, these ingredients are managed to room temperature, and afterward consolidated utilizing a steady mixing movement, called kneading. After bake is applied, the chemical responses make the yeast extend, and at last, the whole mixture rises. After the dough cools, you have a new loaf of bread. The misguided judgment lies in accepting natively constructed bread making is a long and difficult procedure. It might be said, it is in case you're discussing old, the manual way. The consistent checking, estimating, and kneading by itself can take up a decent bit of the day. These automatic gadgets deal with the greater part of these means for you.

The two reasons you ought to consider a bread machine are health and in general expenses. In all honesty, the 4 ingredients recently referenced are the main ones you have to make a loaf of basic white bread. With the present evolved way of life being commanded by high-fructose corn syrup, monosodium glutamate (msg), aspartame, and in part hydrogenated oils, you currently have complete control of what goes into your bread with a bread machine. Second, they are similarly as practical. Simply think about the amount you and your family spend on packaged bread on a yearly premise. You would be amazed your yearly bread costs could in at least match the costs of an entry-level bread machine. Furthermore, the expenses of flour, water, table salt, and yeast joined are truly practically identical to the cost of market and pastry kitchen bread. You might have the option to squeeze out at any rate 5 homemade loaves before getting one of those ingredients once more. As prepackaged bread costs keep on rising, the main rise you'll see is the hot and newly baked dough practically complete in your bread machine.

Bread is a baked food that can be set up from various sorts of dough. The dough is typically made of flour and water. Bread is baked in several shapes, sizes, types, and surfaces. Extents and sorts of flour and different ingredients vary, as do techniques for preparation. Since history, bread has been one of the most essential food, as it is additionally one of the oldest artificial foods. Indeed, individuals were making bread since the beginning of agriculture. Individuals in all societies serve bread in different forms with any dinner of the day. It tends to be eaten as a piece of the dinner or as a different snack.

How Do You Cook Bread?

Bread is typically baked from a wheat flour dough, which is made with yeast and permitted to rise. Commonly, individuals bake bread in the oven. In any case, an ever-increasing number of individuals go to the extraordinary bread machines to bake new bread at home.

What Is A Bread Machine?

A bread machine, or bread maker, is a kitchen appliance for baking bread. The gadget comprises of a bread container or tin with worked in paddles, which is situated in the center of a small uncommon multi-purpose oven.

How Is Bread Machine Made?

As we referenced in the past area, bread makers comprise of a few sections. This machine is essentially a conservative electric oven that holds a single, big bread tin inside. The tin itself is somewhat uncommon – it has an axle at the base that is associated with an electric engine underneath.

A small metal paddle is attached to the pivot at the base of the tin. The paddle is answerable for kneading the dough. The axle itself is secured by a waterproof seal. How about we investigate every one of the bread machine parts in detail:

The top on the bread maker comes either with the review window or without it. The control paddled is likewise situated on the top of the bread machine with the end goal of comfort.

In the center of the lid, there is a steam vent that depletes the steam during the baking procedure. A portion of the bread makers likewise have an air vent on the gadget for air to come inside the tin for the dough to rise

How Does Bread Machine Work?

To start with, you put the kneading paddle inside the tin. At the point when the tin is out of the machine, you can measure the ingredients and load them into the tin.

Subsequently, you simply need to put the container inside the oven (machine), pick the program you wish using the electronic panel, and close the cover. Here the bread maker magic dominates!

One of the primary things the bread machine will do is kneading the dough – you will hear the sounds. In case your bread maker accompanies the viewing window, you can watch the entire procedure of baking, which is very entrancing.

After the kneading stage, everything will go calm for quite a while – the rising stage comes. The machine allows the dough to dough and rise. At that point, there will be another round of kneading and the period of demonstrating.

After the kneading phase, everything will go quiet for some time – the rising phase comes. The machine lets the dough rest and rise. Then, there will be another round of kneading and the phase of proving.

No-Knead Bread Dutch Oven Recipe:

Bread is a baked food that can be set up from various sorts of dough. The dough is regularly made of flour and water. Bread is baked in many shapes, sizes, types, and surfaces. Extents and kinds of flour and different ingredients fluctuate, as do techniques for preparation.

Since history, bread has been one of the most basic foods, as it is additionally one of the most established artificial foods. Indeed, individuals were making bread since the beginning of farming.

Pulling Bread From Inner Pan

Individuals in all societies serve bread in different forms with any dinner of the day. It tends to be eaten as a piece of the feast or as a different snack.

Baked Bread In Machine

At long last, the bread maker' oven will turn on and you will see the steam coming up through the steam vent. Although the typical bread making process is programmed, most machines accompany recipe books that give you various intriguing propelled bread plans.

How To Use A Bread Machine?

Regardless of which bread machine you pick, the baking procedure is the same all over. You load ingredients to the tin, at that point place the bread pan in the machine and pick the essential program.

The average baking process takes anyplace somewhere in the range of 2 and 5 hours, contingent upon the model. Toward the finish of the baking procedure, it is prescribed to put a loaf on a wire rack to chill off before eating it. Much the same as for the hand-made bread recipe, you will require four key ingredients:

- Yeast (or a starter)
- Flour
- Fluid (typically water or milk)
- Salt (for enhancing and to control maturation)

Other than the principal ingredients, you can include some other additional items you need, including raisins, nuts, chocolate chips, and so forth.

While bread baking procedure may appear to be exceptionally primitive and simple, there are a few insights that will make you an ace at bread baking with a bread machine:

Check and adhere to the guidelines/manual. With some bread bakers, the dry ingredients ought to be included first, with others, the wet ingredients go in first.

Besides, when perusing bread baking plans, remember that not the entirety of the bread makers are made equivalent – some item 1 pound loaves, others make 1,5 and 2 pound loaves. A portion of the bread machine models are equipped for baking 3-pound loaves.

When evaluating another recipe, it is important to contrast the measures of ingredients with the plans normally utilized in the bread machine. It is significant not to surpass the limit of the bread machine dish.

Pouring Flour In Bread Maker

If the recipe calls for milk, it isn't prescribed to utilize a deferred mixture cycle.

If you need to make pizza dough in your bread maker, join the warm water, olive oil, salt, flour, and yeast in the bread tin. Set the machine for the 'Pizza Dough' program following the manual of your bread maker. After your dough is baked, you can move it to a softly floured surface for additional handling.

Advantages Of A Bread Machine

While utilizing a bread machine for some may seem like a pointless advance, others don't envision the existence without newly home-baked bread. However, how about we go to the realities – beneath, we indicated the advantages of owning a bread machine.

As a matter of first importance, you can appreciate the newly baked homemade bread. Most bread makers additionally include a clockwork, which permits you to set the bake cycle at a specific time. This capacity is helpful when you need to have sweltering bread toward the beginning of the day for breakfast.

You can control what you eat. By baking bread at home, you can control what parts are coming into your loaf – this choice is exceptionally helpful for individuals with hypersensitivities or for those, who attempt to control the admission of a portion of the ingredients.

It is simple. A few people believe that baking bread at home is muddled and in general, it is a hard procedure. Be that as it may, baking bread with a bread machine is a breeze. You simply pick the ideal choice and unwind - all the mixture, rising, and baking process is going on within the bread maker, which additionally makes it a zero chaos process!

It sets aside you huge amounts of cash in the long haul. If you believe that purchasing bread at a store is modest, you may be mixed up. In turns out that in the long haul, baking bread at home will set aside your cash, particularly if you have some dietary limitations.

Bread machines can create different sorts of bread: entire wheat bread, without gluten bread, rye bread, and several different kinds. They can likewise make pizza dough, pasta dough, jam, and different delightful dishes.

Bread Made In Bread Maker

Great taste and quality. You have to acknowledge it – nothing beats the quality and taste of a new heap of bread. Since you are the person who is making bread, you can ensure that you utilize just the new ingredients and of a high caliber. Homemade bread consistently beats locally acquired bread as far as taste and quality.

What Else Can You Do With A Bread Machine?

We have just referenced that bread maker utilizes are not just restricted to baking various kinds of bread. Here, we might want to investigate some inventive thoughts regarding how to utilize a bread machine.

- You Can Create Your Own Fruit Or Vegetable Butters
- It Is Possible To Make Delicious Tomato Sauce In A Bread Maker
- Bake A Casserole

- Bread Makers Can Bake Cakes

CHAPTER 2: BREAD MACHINES - PROS AND CONS

Initial a tad about the impediments I have encountered:

1. It is noisy. The kneading procedure is a sensible loud undertaking that keeps going 30 brief's aggregate. It is maybe unrealistic to maintain a strategic distance from all the noise from the bread maker, yet if you live in a small condo or house, you can't put it someplace clamor won't trouble you. This implies you will doubtlessly be stirred by the noise if that it begins to knead the dough 3 hours before you need to get up toward the beginning of the day to the brilliant newly baked bread.

2. Holes in the base of the bread. To start with I simply had become accustomed to that there was an opening in my bread yet now I've become used to it, so I won't consider it a disadvantage since it is so insignificant. If individuals have needed to dispose of the bread along these lines, the more likely than not accomplished something incorrectly.

3. Unbaked top. The top is not baked as much as the sides and base, yet it is sufficiently baked. You can't make bread with a brilliant brown covering on top, however, it is baked.

4. Shape. Bread baked in a bread machine is square dislike the bread we know from the pastry kitchen or grocery store. It has taken a touch of becoming accustomed to for me and my family.

5. Bread size. If you are a big family you should know that

standard hardware available presumably doesn't bake large enough bread. A few machines, in any case, are large enough in measure and can cover most family needs; however, the cost is shockingly additionally frequently higher.

Preferences:

1. Cleaning? Exceptionally simple - it's just the baking dish that should be cleaned however since the bread consistently let go effectively, it is frequently superfluous to do other than removing the bit of bread, which sits on the pole to the dough snare. Most bread machines are fitted with Teflon covering and the parts can without much of a stretch be removed, and as a rule, be placed in the dishwasher.

2. Kneading. The bread maker can likewise be utilized to ply dough for different sorts of bread that you would prefer not to bake in the bread maker. I have effectively placed it to knead the dough into buns, treats, and cake.

3. The smell of new bread. It's great that with the clock you can be certain that there is in every case newly baked bread toward the beginning of the day or night with some espresso. The smell of newly baked bread from the baking machine makes it simpler to get up toward the beginning of the day.

4. Baking Master. If you, as I do, love to explore different avenues regarding making different new breads and design new plans, so you feel like a genuine baking champion, at that point a bread maker is a flat out hit. So far I have attempted with Graham flour, split wheat loaves, pecans, rye bread mixture.

15

5. Aside from the clamor, I'm extremely content with my bread maker. It makes superb bread. It is anything but difficult to clean, and as I stated, staggeringly simple to set up. One will before long locate their preferred plans, but on the other hand, it's very amusing to try different things with kneading/raise/bake times and ingredients.

Tips On Getting The Best Out Of Your Bread Machine

Individuals are regularly baffled with the outcomes they get when utilizing their bread machine and inevitably quit utilizing it. This is a genuine disgrace as there's nothing superior to healthy, home-baked bread, and a bread maker should make home baking fun and simple. In this way, in case you're making them the issues with your machine, don't surrender. Here are a few hints that will, ideally, help you along.

The best tip on utilizing a bread machine is before you ever use it. Continuously take a couple of seconds to deliberately peruse the guidance manual that goes with the machine. Give uncommon care to the attention and upkeep segment. Perpetually, there is a 'breaking in' cycle that bakes the machine for use. This is generally done by running a cycle with no dough. Never keep away from this progression.

A minor bother is evacuating the mixture paddle after the bread has baked. Many whine that the paddle is 'baked in' and evacuating it is a genuine problem. You can make this simpler by first spreading some margarine on the paddle; you can likewise utilize olive oil. Never attempt to remove the paddle utilizing a blade or other metal item as this will scratch the non-stick covering of the dish.

A few bakers state in the guidance manual that the paddle and container can be placed in a dishwasher. Never do this. Rather, put warm sudsy water within the container; don't submerge the entire of the dish in water. Leave the pan to douse for fifteen minutes and afterward void water and delicately wipe down with a dish material.

Many gripe that the loaf soaks in the center, although they've carefully followed the maker's recipe. Right off the bat, baking bread is as much as a workmanship as it is science. Elevation, air temperature, dampness, and newness of ingredients can fluctuate. You may need to test and change the recipe somewhat. A listing loaf is generally the aftereffect of there being an excess of water in the mixture. Have a go at decreasing the sum. When adjusting the ingredients, bring estimations and record them so you remember and can rehash the recipe. If this issue proceeds with it might be a direct result of the yeast

The outside can here and there appear to be excessively hard or thick. This is typically because the mixture is excessively dry. Adding somewhat more water to the mixture can fix this issue. You can likewise utilize milk rather than water, or utilize the sandwich cycle - if your machine has one.

If that the top of the portion isn't caramelizing equally all finished, have a go at setting a bit of aluminum - sparkly side down - on the portion before baking.

If that your loaves are rising excessively, yet you're utilizing the suggested measure of yeast, have a go at including somewhat more salt. Brace, represses the development of yeast, excessively small and the yeast duplicates excessively, excessively quick, making the portion over the rise, breakdown, or potentially have a paddle lopsided surface.

Sugar works the inverse to salt; it takes care of the yeast. Brown sugar can supplant white granulated - simply supplant it with a similar amount. Nectar can likewise be utilized as a sugar substitution however make certain to lessen the measure of fluid by a similar measure of nectar utilized.

Continuously place the ingredients in the dish in the request suggested by the manufacturer. Never let the yeast contact the fluids - you ought to be progressively careful this doesn't occur when utilizing the postponed clock cycle.

The above are only some fundamental bread machine tips. They are the most significant ones to follow to guarantee you get an ideal portion without fail.

Bread Machine Recipes Do it All For You

Bread machine plans give the most straightforward approach to appreciate new hot bread from the solace of home. You'll be glad to realize that the machine does the entirety of the work for you! You essentially hurl the necessary ingredients into the machine and leave.

After three hours you'll get the chance to appreciate a new hot loaf that has been making your mouth water. For what reason would you ever need to utilize something else? Certainly, planning and working the dough yourself is an incredible method to assuage pressure, however, the alternate way of utilizing a bread machine is one that can't be

18

coordinated. What will innovation consider straightaway?

The excellence of such machines, for example, the Panasonic SD YD250 programmed bread maker is that they are completely planned with a similar reason; to create a hot, succulent loaf of bread that is baked to eat the second the machine has killed. You can make a big assortment of loaf items too.

You don't need to restrict yourself to a customary loaf of the white one. Why not attempt homemade cinnamon jobs, sticky buns, moves, portion sticks, or even pastas? It will be an incredible treat for your whole family and you can even make some baked treats to provide for companions. They will most unquestionably be dazzled with your culinary abilities.

Most loaf bakers have free bread machine plans that are incorporated with the buy. There are sweet bread plans, for example, those utilized for sticky buns and cinnamon jobs. There are move plans for those magnificently flaky, French croissants, with the delightfully delicate inside and the rich outside layer.

It is a rewarding blessing on the maker. To make things considerably simpler, there are box mixtures that you can purchase that take the entirety of the mystery out of estimating. Everything you do is purchase the crate mixture in the store and follow the directions. They are structured particularly for a bread maker machine. No longer will you need to work and shape the dough yourself. The machine accomplishes all the work for you!

You are insane if you don't go out and quickly buy a bread-making machine. The Zojirushi bread maker is an incredible brand and it accompanies free bread machine plans so you can appreciate all the extraordinary breads you might need.

You will be astonished at the fact that it is so natural to create a new loaf thusly. To make things significantly simpler, get yourself a container mixture. Your companions will be delighted to get a loaf of your homemade loaf as an awesome blessing.

CHAPTER 3: HOMEMADE BREAD RECIPE

Who doesn't cherish newly homemade bread? If you concur, we got this incredibly delicious and simple homemade bread recipe only for you. You will require:

- cup warm water (110 degrees F/45degrees C)
- 2 tablespoons white sugar
- 1(1/4 ounce) bundle bread machine yeast (2-1/4 teaspoons)
- 2 tablespoons softened spread
- 2 tablespoons oil (can utilize 4 tablespoons of oil or softened spread)
- 3cups white bread flour
- 1teaspoon salt

Headings

1. Spot the water into the bread tin. Sprinkle the sugar and the yeast over the water. Leave the mixture for 10 minutes. Include the liquefied margarine, oil, flour, and salt.
2. Pick the Basic or White Bread setting on your bread machine and press start. Bake for 3 - 4 hours.
3. How To Make Gluten-Free Bread?

To make gluten-free bread in your bread machine, you will require the accompanying:

- 1 1/2tablespoons dry yeast, granules (or Bread Maker yeast)
- 1teaspoon vinegar (or dough enhancer)
- 2 1/2 teaspoons thickener (or guar gum)
- 2/3cup powdered milk (or 1/2 nondairy substitute)
- 2 cups rice flour
- 1/2cup potato starch
- 3 tablespoons sugar
- 3 eggs, room temperature
- 1 1/2teaspoons egg substitute (discretionary)
- 1/2cup custard flour
- 1 1/2teaspoons salt
- 1 2/3cups tepid water
- 3 tablespoons sugar
- 1 2/3cups tepid water
- 4 tablespoons spread, dissolved (or margarine)

Directions

You can mix the majority of the ingredients in the baking container of the bread maker as proposed by your manual. Utilize the white bread setting at medium outside (if that you have these settings). Bake for 3 - 4 hours.

CHAPTER 4: BREAD MACHINE COUNTRY WHITE BREAD

This straightforward bread machine white bread recipe comes through with a charming, chewy surface. It's delightful as toast for breakfast or uses it to make incredible sandwiches, grilled or not. This white bread loaf doesn't have many air gaps or air pockets, yet the flavor and surface are brilliant. You can make this bread on a fast or speedy cycle, yet it could likewise be made on the standard cycle with somewhat less yeast (around 2 teaspoons).

Ingredients

- 2 1/2 teaspoons bread machine yeast (fast or moment)
- 1 tablespoon in addition to 1 teaspoon olive oil
- 1/2 teaspoons sugar
- 1 teaspoon salt
- 1/2 cups water (tepid)
- 2 1/2 cups universally handy flour
- 1 cup bread flour
- 1/4 teaspoon baking pop

Steps to Make It

1. Add the entirety of the ingredients to your bread machine pan in the request suggested by your bread machine maker.
2. Set to the brisk or fast setting and medium outside layer. Push start.

3. When baked, turn the bread out onto a rack to cool.

4. Cut and appreciate!

Tip

At the point when your bread machine has been kneading for a couple of moments, check the dough. If it appears to be excessively solid, include a tad of water and keep checking until it appears to be sufficiently delicate. If that excessively wet, include more flour in limited quantities until it is by all accounts delicate yet not sticky.

CHAPTER 5: WHOLE WHEAT BREAD FROM A BREAD MACHINE

Homemade bread is delicious, yet if that you are attempting to adhere to your eating routine, you might be advised to maintain a strategic distance from it. What's more, if that you have a bread maker at home, you make certain to be enticed. Why not bake more beneficial bread? Appreciate this entire wheat bread made in the bread machine.

Ingredients

- 1/2 cup in addition to 2 tablespoons water
- 2 tablespoons vegetable oil
- 4 1/4 cups entire wheat flour
- 3 tablespoons nonfat dry milk
- 2 teaspoons dynamic dry yeast
- 2 teaspoons salt
- 1/3 cup brown sugar (pressed)

Steps to Make It

1. Assemble the ingredients.
2. Spot ingredients in bread pan in the request recorded or as per the maker's directions.
3. While including the yeast last, make a small well with your finger to put the yeast. This will guarantee the best possible planning of the yeast response.
4. Utilize the Whole Wheat or Timed Cycle, or follow the maker's

directions.

5. Appreciate!

CHAPTER 6: MULTIGRAIN LOAF BREAD

Utilize your most loved multigrain oat in this tasty bread machine recipe, which is staggeringly acceptable toasted. Multigrain Loaf is brimming with flavor and surface, and its remarkable spread with your preferred jam or jam or with whipped nectar for breakfast. Likewise use it to make sandwiches, particularly with cut meal hamburgers or chicken. Or on the other hand, make barbecued cheese sandwiches for a great mixture of softened and gooey cheese and fresh and crunchy bread.

Bread machines were extremely popular around 10 years prior, however they have fallen out of fashion. We despite everything think they are an extraordinary esteem and can give you homemade bread with next to no effort on your part. So pull yours out of the pantry and make this recipe!

Bread machines are every one of the somewhat extraordinary, so to utilize yours accurately, ensure you follow the maker's directions for including ingredients, kneading, timing, and baking. Peruse the guidance booklet to ensure you see how to utilize the machine before you start. At that point appreciate the flavorful outcomes.

Ingredients

- 1/4 cups water
- 2 tablespoons spread (relaxed)

- 1 cup seven-grain or multigrain oat
- 3 tablespoons brown sugar
- 1/4 teaspoons salt
- 2 1/2 teaspoons bread machine yeast
- 1/3 cups bread flour
- 1/3 cups entire wheat flour

Steps to Make It

1. Spot the water, mellowed margarine, bread flour, entire wheat flour, seven-grain oat, brown sugar, salt, and bread machine yeast in the bread machine pan in the request suggested by the machine maker.
2. Select the Whole Wheat or Basic/White Cycle.
3. Utilize the Medium or Light Crust Color choice and start the machine.
4. Let the machine mix the dough, ply the bread, let the dough rise, and bake the bread.
5. Remove the bread from the bread machine when it's set and let it cool totally on a wire rack.

CHAPTER 7: BREAD MACHINE MILK AND HONEY BREAD

This is delightful homemade yeast bread, and the bread machine makes planning nearly hands-free. It's great bread for sandwiches and toast, with a light sweetness that supplements an assortment of flavors. If that you've been purchasing loaves of the run of the mill white bread at the store, you will cherish making it yourself. The smell of the bread, as it bakes, is itself worth the effort.

You should counsel the guidelines for your bread machine, as models can contrast in the request in which you include the ingredients. Most models have composed guidelines; however, they are additionally accessible on the web, alongside instructional recordings.

The yeast is one ingredient that requires exceptional thoughtfulness regarding its "utilization by" date. Make certain to keep it refrigerated or frozen before use. If that you have a kind other than dynamic dry yeast, utilize these changes: 2 teaspoons dynamic dry yeast equal 1/2 teaspoons fast rise, moment, or bread machine yeast.

You can likewise make dough for supper moves rather than a loaf, utilizing the dough cycle on your machine.

Ingredients

- 1 cup in addition to 1 tablespoon milk
- 3 cups bread flour

- 1/2 teaspoons salt
- 2 teaspoons dynamic dry yeast
- 3 tablespoons nectar
- 3 tablespoons spread (dissolved)

Steps to Make It

1. Accumulate the ingredients.
2. Include ingredients (milk, nectar, spread, flour, salt, and yeast) to the bread machine dish in the request suggested by your bread machine maker.
3. Pick the essential or white bread setting and the medium crust setting.
4. Start the bread machine.
5. Remove the hot loaf when it is done. If that you leave it in the machine it can get soggy. Spot it on a wire rack to cool totally.
6. Once cooled, cut the bread and serve or store it for some time later.
7. Putting away Your Milk and Honey Bread

If that you will utilize the bread throughout the following three days, you can store it at room temperature in foil, plastic wraps, or a plastic pack. Pick a cool, dry spot to keep your bread loaf.

If that you have to store the bread for more, freeze the cooled loaf in a cooler pack. Mark the sack with the date, substance, and a "utilization by" date three months later. At the point when you need to utilize it, remove it from the cooler and permit it to defrost at room temperature for 60 minutes

CHAPTER 8: SWEET POTATO ROLLS

These delicate, scrumptious sweet potato yeast rolls are kneaded in the bread machine, making them a snap to plan, shape, and bake.

The basic mix of ingredients makes around 2 dozen force separated rolls. You don't just have a bread machine to make these rolls. Knead the dough by hand or with your stand mixer if you'd like.

Ingredients

- 2 medium sweet potatoes (1 cup, squashed)
- 3/4 cup milk
- 4 cups universally handy flour (18 ounces)
- 4 tablespoons sugar
- 1 teaspoon salt
- 2 1/4 teaspoons dynamic dry yeast
- 3 tablespoons margarine (dissolved, in addition to extra to top turns out of the oven)
- 1 big egg (beaten)

Steps to Make It

1. Accumulate the ingredients.
2. Strip 2 medium sweet potatoes and cut them into cubes.
3. Heat a pot of salted water to the point of boiling over high warmth.
4. Add the sweet potato cubes to the bubbling water and low the warmth to low. Spread the pan and cook for around 20 minutes,

31

or until delicate.

5. Drain well and mash.

6. Cool totally and measure 1 cup for the recipe.

7. Add all ingredients to the bread machine in the request recommended by the maker.

8. Utilize the essential dough cycle. At the point when the cycle completes, detach pieces from the dough to make balls, and a spot in a lubed 9-inch square baking dish so they're simply contacting however not very close. (around 1 3/4 ounces each to get around 24 rolls)

9. Cover the rolls with a cloth and let rise for around 45 minutes in a warm, without draft place.

10. Preheat oven to 375 F.

11. Bake in the oven for around 20 to 23 minutes, until pleasantly sautéed.

12. Brush the tops with liquefied or relaxed spread while they're hot.

Appreciate!

CHAPTER 9: DELICATE PRETZELS FROM THE BREAD MACHINE

Delicate pretzels are a snap to make when you utilize the bread machine to make the dough. Although you'll need to trust that the dough will be baked, this delicate pretzel is excessively simple for children to make.

Ingredients

- 1/2 cups water
- 1 teaspoon fit salt
- 1 tablespoon light brown sugar (solidly stuffed)
- 3 1/2 cups flour
- 2 teaspoon dynamic dry yeast
- 2 quarts water
- 1/3 cup baking pop
- Kosher salt

Steps to Make It

1. Spot the initial five ingredients in your bread machine in the request indicated by the maker.
2. Set the machine to the dough cycle.
3. At the point when a cycle is finished, turn the dough out onto a delicately floured surface, and let it rest a couple of moments. In the meantime, preheat the oven to 475 F. Get out two baking sheets, and spot a rack over a third baking sheet.
4. Separation dough into 12 to14 equivalent pieces. Turn each

piece out to a 15-inch rope.

5. Make a U with each rope, at that point cross the finishes. Get the finishes and turn, at that point fold up to make a pretzel shape. Squeeze to seal. To perceive what this resembles, look at this bit by bit instructional exercise on the best way to make delicate pretzels. Spot the pretzels on the salted baking sheets.

6. Spot the 2 quarts of water in a big pan. Bake to the point of boiling. Include the baking pop; at that point decrease the warmth to a stew.

7. Slide 2 to 3 pretzels one after another into the baking soft drink shower. Let them stew around 2 minutes. Utilize an opened spoon to remove the pretzels. Move to the cooling rack. Sprinkle with legitimate salt.

8. At the point when the entirety of the pretzels have come out of the baking soft drink shower, move them to the salted baking sheets.

9. Bake 8 to 12 minutes until brilliant brown.

CHAPTER 10: NUTTY SPREAD BREAD

Did you ever think to put nutty spread inside your bread rather than on top? This rich bread is ideal for breakfast, toasted with jam! You could include progressively nutty spread when the bread is toasted, for the ideal nutty spread and jam sandwich.

Likewise, with all breads, be certain you measure cautiously and utilize the best ingredients. Ensure that your yeast is new. Continuously follow lapse dates on yeast. There's nothing more terrible than making a loaf of bread, just to have a disappointment because the yeast has terminated. What's more, cautiously follow the directions that accompanied your bread machine.

Ingredients

- 1 cup in addition to 1 tablespoon water
- 3 tablespoons brown sugar
- 1 teaspoon salt
- 2 teaspoons yeast (bread machine)
- 1/2 cup nutty spread
- 3 cups flour (bread)

Steps to Make It

1. Accumulate the ingredients.
2. Estimating cautiously, place the water, nutty spread, bread

flour, brown sugar, salt, and bread machine yeast in the bread machine in the request suggested by the maker.

3. Select "Sweet" or "Essential/White" cycle. Use "Medium" or "Light Crust Color" and turn the machine on. At the point when the bread is done, it ought to be dark gold color and should sound empty when you tap it with your fingers. You can likewise test the temperature of the bread; it ought to be around 210 F.

4. Cautiously remove the bread from the bread machine container and cool it on a wire rack.

Tips

Continuously read the booklet that accompanies your machines before you use them.

This bread, similar to every homemade bread, doesn't keep well. I like to cut it and freeze it with bits of material paper between the cuts. That way you can pull out several cuts and toast them for breakfast to eat on the run.

CHAPTER 11: BREAD MACHINE ONION BREAD

If you are searching for a simple onion bread to add to your meal, you can't turn go wrong with this Onion Bread Recipe for use in the bread machine. This recipe utilizes an onion soup mixture as its primary ingredient, a basic thing huge numbers of us as of now have in our pantry.

Ingredients

- 1-1/2 cups water
- 2 tablespoons in addition to 2 teaspoons margarine
- 2 tablespoons in addition to 2 teaspoons nonfat dry milk
- 2 teaspoons dynamic dry yeast
- 3-4 tablespoons dry onion soup mixture
- 1-1/2 teaspoons salt
- 1 tablespoon in addition to 1-1/2 teaspoons sugar
- 4 cups bread flour

Steps to Make It

1. Place ingredients in bread pan all together recorded or as manufacturer's directions.
2. The onion soup mixture is included at the fruit and nut signal. Depending upon your machine this could be somewhere in the range of 30 to 40 minutes into the cycle.

Tips

Keep in mind, while including the yeast last, make a small well with your finger to put the yeast. This will guarantee the best possible timing of the yeast reaction.

This bread is baked at the Basic (Standard) or Timed Cycle, or as manufacturer's directions.

CHAPTER 12: BREAD MACHINE HAMBURGER BUNS

Bread machine cheeseburger buns are an incredible decision in case you're searching for a snappy homemade bun for burgers or hotdogs. The machine makes mixing and kneading a breeze—they're nearly as simple as hurrying to the store and getting locally acquired buns.

The recipe makes around 8 huge hamburger buns, or you can make small buns for sliders. Brush the buns with a straightforward egg wash not long before they go into the oven and sprinkle with sesame seeds or poppy seeds. The egg wash will help produce a pleasantly seared top and will give the seeds something to adhere to. The egg white and water egg wash makes the covering somewhat firmer and includes sparkle. For a delicate outside, sparkle, and a touch of extra brilliant color make the egg wash with egg yolk with 1 tablespoon of milk or cream or an entire egg with 1 tablespoon of water.

Your Handy Guide to Baking with a Bread Machine

Ingredients

- 1/3 cups water
- 2 tablespoons nonfat milk powder
- 4 cups generally useful flour (in addition to additional for kneading)
- 2 teaspoons salt
- 1 bundle dynamic dry yeast (around 2 1/2 teaspoons)

39

- Cornmeal
- 1 egg white (rushed with 1 tablespoon of water)
- Discretionary: 2 tablespoons sesame seeds (or poppy seeds)
- 2 tablespoons shortening
- 2 1/2 to 3 tablespoons sugar

Steps to Make It

1. Accumulate the ingredients.
2. Include the water and non-fat milk powder to the bread machine followed by the flour. Include the shortening followed by the sugar, salt, and yeast. Set to the "dough" cycle.
3. At the point when the dough cycle completes, turn the dough out onto a floured paddled and punch it down. Knead 4 or multiple times; include somewhat more flour as you work if important to shield it from adhering to your hands or the load up.
4. Spread the dough with a spotless dishcloth and let rest for around 30 minutes in a without draft place.
5. Softly oil a big baking sheet; sprinkle with cornmeal. On the other hand, line the baking sheet with material paper and sprinkle with cornmeal.
6. Pat the dough into a circle and cut into 8 even wedges. Structure each wedge into a ball at that point straighten into a smooth and genuinely even circle, somewhat greater than a burger. On the other hand, shape each wedge into long, limited shapes for a wiener or hotdog buns, or cut each wedge down the middle and shape into smaller buns for sliders or party sandwiches.

40

7. Arrange the dough pieces on the baking sheet around 2 inches separated and let rest for around 20 minutes.

8. Preheat the oven to 375 F (190 C/Gas 5).

9. Brush the buns softly with the egg wash (egg and water mixture). Whenever wanted, sprinkle with sesame seeds or poppy seeds.

10. Bake the buns for around 18 minutes, or until the buns are pleasantly cooked.

11. Let cool before serving.

CHAPTER 13: QUINOA OATMEAL BREAD IN A BREAD MACHINE

Include this nutritious quinoa cereal bread to your assortment of bread machine plans. The mixture of quinoa—a high-protein grain—oats, wheat, and bread flours, buttermilk, and nectar brings about a tasty, healthy bread with a nutty flavor and chewy surface.

Crude quinoa grains should be cooked before adding them to the bread dough, or you can substitute quinoa chips (a baked type of quinoa intended to be eaten as hot oat which looks like oats) for the cooked quinoa and kill that additional progression.

Ingredients

- 1/3 cup uncooked quinoa, or 1/2 cup quinoa pieces
- 2/3 cup water (for cooking quinoa grains)
- 1 cup buttermilk
- 1 tablespoon nectar
- 4 tablespoons (1/2 stick) unsalted margarine
- 1/2 cup brisk cooking oats
- 1/2 cup entire wheat flour
- 1/2 cups bread flour
- 1 teaspoon salt
- 1 tablespoon sugar

Steps to Make It

1. Assemble the ingredients.
2. To a pan, include the quinoa and spread it with the water. (If that utilizing quinoa drops rather than crude quinoa, avoid this progression). Bake to the point of boiling and cook for 5 minutes, secured. Turn off the warmth and let quinoa sit, secured, for 10 minutes.
3. Check your bread machine directions for the right request to include the ingredients. Add all the rest of the ingredients to the bread machine, including cooked quinoa (or quinoa drops).
4. Program machine for a whole-grain loaf and bake.
5. Let the bread cool for 15 minutes before cutting.
6. Cut, serve, and appreciate!

Tips

Significantly, you know about how your bread machine functions before you jump into a recipe. Verify the limit of your machine; some make 1-pound loaves while others make 1/2-to 2-pound loaves, so when making another recipe, you should contrast and the estimations of a recipe you know about to ensure your machine can deal with it. There are likewise particulars while including the ingredients; certain machines require including the wet ingredients first while others require the dry.

Quinoa bread is a thick loaf you can appreciate with your preferred spreads, for example, nut margarine, spread, jam, jam, cream cheese, chutney, and that's just the beginning. You can likewise serve cuts to go with soups and stews.

Store the bread in a water/air proof sack at room temperature to keep it new. It should most recent 3 days at room temperature, an extra 2 days whenever refrigerated. Monitor it for any mold development and dispose of when you see the shape. You can likewise freeze the loaf, fixed in a hermetically sealed pack, for a small while.

If that you don't have a bread machine, you can make nectar quinoa bread as it was done in the good 'old days.

CHAPTER 14: BREAD MACHINE HERB AND PARMESAN BREAD RECIPE

This superb, sweet-smelling herb and Parmesan loaf is a phenomenal bread to present with lasagna, spaghetti, or soup. I utilized new oregano, chives, a small basil, and rosemary. If you decide to utilize dried herbs, use around 1 tablespoon of dried leaf herbs.

Ingredients

- 1/3 cups tepid water
- 2 tablespoons olive oil
- 4 cups bread flour
- 1 insufficient teaspoon salt
- 1 tablespoon sugar
- 4 tablespoons Parmesan cheese (ground)
- 2 1/4 teaspoons dynamic dry yeast
- 2 cloves squashed garlic
- 3 tablespoons new herbs (slashed, for example, a mixture of basil, chives, oregano, and rosemary)

Steps to Make It

1. Add all ingredients to your bread machine in the order suggested by the maker.
2. Bake on the essential cycle, medium coverage.

3. Makes one 2-pound loaf.

Chapter 15: Jewish Bread Machine Challah

Ingredients

- 1/2 teaspoons salt
- 1 huge egg (beaten)
- 1 huge egg yolk (beaten)
- 4 2/3 cups flour (bread)
- 1/4 teaspoons yeast (moment or bread machine)
- 1 huge egg (beaten for egg wash)
- Discretionary: sesame or poppy seeds
- 1 cup water (tepid)
- 1/2 cup nectar
- 2 1/2 tablespoons oil (vegetable)

Steps to Make It

1. Include salt, egg, egg yolk, water, nectar, and oil to the bread dish. Spoon flour on the liquid. Include yeast.
2. Select the Basic/White or Sweet cycle and the Light Crust setting and press Start.
3. Toward the beginning of the last rise, press Pause. Remove dough from bread dish, move to a floured surface and punch down delicately.
4. Separation dough into thirds. Fold every third into a 10-inch long rope. Spread the three ropes out corresponding to one

47

another on a floured surface so they are exceptionally close, yet not contacting. Twist ropes together cozily. Fold finishes under framing an oval portion.

5. Brush mesh with beaten egg and sprinkle with sesame or poppy seeds, whenever wanted, squeezing the seeds into the dough.

6. Evacuate kneading paddle(s) from the bread dish. Spot interlace in pan and press Start to proceed with the cycle.

7. The machine will reveal to you when the bread is finished. Evacuate to a wire rack to cool totally before cutting.

CHAPTER 16: BREAD MACHINE SWEET POTATO BREAD

This simple sweet potato yeast bread is mixed and baked in the bread machine. A couple of flavors, dark brown sugar, and a small vanilla add flavor to this bread.

If that you utilize canned sweet potatoes in this recipe, wash off any abundance syrup before you crush them.

Add raisins or cleaved walnuts to this bread if you like. Follow to your bread machine makers' guidelines for including ingredients.

Ingredients

- 1/2 cup in addition to 2 tablespoons water (5 ounces)
- 1 teaspoon vanilla concentrate
- 1 cup plain squashed sweet potatoes
- 4 cups bread flour
- 1/3 cup dark brown sugar
- 1/2 teaspoons salt
- 2 teaspoons dynamic dry yeast
- 2 tablespoons dry milk powder
- raisins or cleaved walnuts, discretionary
- 1/4 teaspoon each ground nutmeg and cinnamon
- 2 tablespoons spread

Steps to Make It

49

1. Add ingredients as per the manufacture's proposed request.
2. Utilize white bread setting, light outside.
3. Whenever wanted, include raisins or walnuts when your bread machine blares for extra ingredients.

CHAPTER 17: BREAD MACHINE KALAMATA OLIVE BREAD

This Kalamata olive bread recipe makes a big loaf of bread in a bread machine. It is a simple arrangement, and the olives make it a great bread to present with a spaghetti supper. The dried basil adds an extra homegrown flavor to the portion.

If you have a container of Kalamata olives, you ought to have a lot of saline solution. If you are purchasing your olives from an olive bar at the grocery store, make certain to get saline solution alongside the olives.

The aroma of the basil and Kalamata olives make your kitchen smell wonderful while it's baking, and it's delectable. It is an extraordinary option in contrast to garlic bread to present with any Italian-propelled dinner. You needn't bother with any margarine on this bread, it is tasty enough just cut. It is great to present with soups, for example, minestrone or Tuscan bean soup.

Ingredients

- 1/3 to 1/2 cup saline solution from olives
- 1 cup warm water (enough to make 1/2 cups when joined with saline solution)
- 2 tablespoons olive oil
- 1/2 teaspoons salt
- 2 tablespoons sugar

- 1/2 teaspoons basil (dried leaf)
- 2 teaspoons dynamic dry yeast
- 1/2 to 2/3 cup olives (finely slashed Kalamata, around 2 dozen pitted olives)
- 3 cups bread flour
- 1 2/3 cups entire wheat flour

Steps to Make It

1. Put the olive saline solution in a 2-cup measure; add warm water to make 1/2 cups volume.
2. Put all ingredients aside from the olives in the bread machine as per your maker's favored request.
3. Pick the fundamental or wheat setting on your bread machine.
4. Include olives at the signal demonstrating time to include mixture in ingredients.
5. At the point when your loaf is done baking, cut it and appreciate it without anyone else, with spread, or with olive oil.

CHAPTER 18: BROILED GARLIC BREAD FOR THE BREAD MACHINE

Broiled garlic bread for the bread machine has an after taste like toasted garlic bread. It's flavorful and simple to make.

Ingredients

- 1 bulb broiled garlic
- 3 tablespoons spread
- 4 cloves garlic (minced)
- 1 teaspoon salt
- 1/2 teaspoon garlic powder
- 1-1/2 teaspoons bread machine yeast
- 1/2 cup water
- 1/3 cup milk
- 2-3/4 cups bread flour
- 1/3 cup Parmesan cheese (ground)
- 2 tablespoons sugar

Steps to Make It

1. Accumulate the ingredients.
2. Get ready-cooked garlic. After crushing garlic out of cloves, squash somewhat and measure 1/4 cup for the 1-1/2 lb. recipe.
3. In a small microwave-safe dish, add margarine and minced

garlic. Microwave on high for 1-2 minutes until garlic is fragrant.

4. Spot all ingredients except for the simmered garlic in the bread machine dish in the request suggested by the maker.

5. Tune in to the machine as it kneads; if that it sounds unpleasant or stressing includes all the more warm water. If that the dough is excessively wet or delicate, include more flour. This is a regular practice in bread machines since flour ingests pretty much water contingent upon the developing states of the wheat and the locale where it was developed.

6. Include crushed garlic at the Raisin/Nut sign or 5-10 minutes before the last kneading cycle closes. Select the Basic/White cycle and utilize Medium or Light Crust Color. Try not to utilize postpone cycles.

CHAPTER 19: BREAD MACHINE HONEY BUTTERMILK BREAD

This nectar buttermilk bread is a great bread machine loaf. Simply add the entirety of the ingredients to the machine and press the beginning catch.

Nectar and buttermilk give this yeast bread incredible flavor and surface.

Ingredients

- 2 teaspoons yeast
- 3 cups bread flour
- 3 teaspoons margarine (mollified)
- 3 tablespoons nectar
- 1/2 cup water
- 1/2 teaspoons salt
- 3/4 cup buttermilk (very much shaken)

Topping:

- sesame seeds

Steps to Make It

To Make a Loaf

1. Assemble the ingredients.

2. Put all ingredients in the bread machine in the order proposed by the bread machine maker. Pick essential or white bread and light or medium covering setting.
3. Utilize the dough cycle and shape the bread into a loaf.
4. Spot it on a lubed baking sheet or in a loaf container and brush with an egg wash made with 1 big egg white and 2 teaspoons of water. Whenever wanted, sprinkle the loaf with sesame seeds.
5. Sesame seeds on nectar buttermilk bread loaf
6. Bake at 375 F for around 30 minutes, or until the bread sounds empty when tapped delicately on the base.

To Make Rolls

1. Put all ingredients in the bread machine, in the request proposed by the bread machine maker. Pick essential or white bread and light or medium outside layer setting.
2. Utilize the dough cycle.
3. At that point knead once more, including some flour if the dough is sticky.
4. Shape into rolls and permit to rise until multiplied in mass.
5. You can utilize an egg wash and sprinkle with seeds of your decision; poppy, sesame, or caraway.
6. Bake at 375 F until delicately cooked.

CHAPTER 20: BREAD MACHINE CAJUN BREAD

This bread machine loaf is made with the expansion of garlic, onion, pepper, and Cajun or Creole seasonings. The bread has an astonishing flavor and makes marvelous sandwiches.

Utilize the dough cycle if you like to make moves for sandwiches and follow the move variety. To make a 1/2 pound loaf, just duplicate the ingredients by 1.5.

Ingredients

- 1/2 cup water
- 1/4 cup onion (hacked)
- 1/4 cup green chile pepper (slashed)
- 1 tablespoon sugar
- 1 teaspoon Cajun (or Creole) flavoring
- Inadequate 1/2 teaspoon salt (use around 3/4 teaspoon if your Cajun flavoring is sans salt)
- 1 teaspoon dynamic dry yeast
- 2 teaspoons garlic (hacked finely)
- 2 teaspoons spread (delicate)
- 2 cups bread flour

Steps to Make It

Portion Instructions

1. Measure all ingredients into the machine as per the manufacture's direction for including ingredients.
2. Select the essential/white bread cycle. Utilize medium or dim outside layer shading. (Try not to utilize defer cycles.)
3. Remove from container and cool on wire rack.

Sandwich Roll Instructions

1. Put the ingredients in the bread machine and pick the dough sets.
2. Remove the dough from the machine, partition it into around 10 to 12 segments, and shape into rolls.
3. Spot them on a huge daintily lubed or material paper-lined baking sheet.
4. Spread with a sodden kitchen towel and let the moves rise for around 35 to 45 minutes, or until multiplied.
5. Not long before baking, whisk an egg white with 1 tablespoon of water and brush over each roll.
6. Sprinkle with sesame seeds, whenever wanted.
7. Bake in a preheated 350 F oven for around 15 minutes, or until brilliant brown.

CHAPTER 21: BREAD MACHINE COCOA BREAD

If you have a craving for a loaf that has a smidgen of chocolate goodness, this recipe is anything but difficult to make with your bread machine. Cocoa gives this bread machine recipe and unpretentious chocolate enhance. It's not very sweet and is ideal for breakfast when it's toasted and slathered with raspberry jam.

If you need to layer on the chocolate enhance, consider Nutella or a small nut margarine and nectar or jam. Check out it with a smear of natural product improved cream cheese.

Cocoa bread is extraordinary for a sentimental breakfast for Valentine's Day. In any case, think past that to a birthday or anniversary brunch with that unique individual or even a morning meal group or informal breakfast for the area, companions, or business. If that you have a toaster in the lunchroom at work, you may carry it along to share with your office mates for a team surprise.

Since this recipe utilizes eggs and milk, don't utilize this bread machine recipe with a delayed start clock as you don't need the ingredients sitting unrefrigerated as microorganisms could multiply. Remember this sanitation safety measure.

Ingredients

- 1 cup milk

- 1 egg, in addition to 1 yolk
- 3 tablespoons canola oil
- 1 teaspoon vanilla concentrate
- 1/2 cup brown sugar
- 1/3 cup cocoa powder
- 1 tablespoon imperative wheat gluten
- 2 1/2 teaspoons bread machine yeast
- 1 teaspoon salt
- 3 cups bread flour

Steps to Make It

1. Add ingredients as trained in your bread machine manual. Set the programmable settings for "essential" or "white bread," the loaf size for "1/2 pounds" and the outside layer color for "medium."
2. At the point when the bread is done cooking, remove it quickly from the container and let it cool totally on a cooling rack before cutting.
3. Store the rest of the bread enveloped by plastic wrap for 1 to 2 days.

CHAPTER 22: OATS BREAD WITH MOLASSES AND HONEY

The automatic bread machine removes the drudgery from homemade bread-baking. If that you like a traditionally molded loaf or round loaf, you can utilize the machine to mixture and ply the dough and afterward finish it in a regular dish or on a baking sheet.

This simple bread machine oats bread is enhanced with a mixture of nectar and molasses. It's an astonishing toasting bread, and it makes incredible sandwiches. You'll adore this daintily improved bread with jam toward the beginning of the day, and it is especially acceptable with baked beans.

Ingredients

- 1 cup water (bubbling)
- 2 tablespoons spread
- 1/2 cup oats (antiquated)
- 1 huge egg (delicately beaten)
- 3 cups bread flour
- 2 teaspoons yeast (sprinkled over flour)
- 1/2 teaspoons salt
- 3 tablespoons nectar
- 1 tablespoon dark molasses

Steps to Make It

1. Put the oats in a mixing bowl. Pour the 1 cup of bubbling water over the oats, and put in a safe spot.
2. At the point when oats have cooled however are still somewhat warm (around 105 F to 110 F), move them to the bread machine container. Ensure they are not much hotter, or the warmth could kill the yeast.
3. Add the rest of the ingredients as per your bread machine maker's manual.
4. Bake on light setting.
5. The recipe makes a 1/2-pound loaf.

CHAPTER 23: BREAD MACHINE OREGANO AND ROMANO CHEESE BREAD

Verla's bread machine herb bread is overly simple to get ready, and it is the ideal bread for a spaghetti or lasagna dinner. You should bake this bread only for the superb fragrance!

I've made the bread with Parmesan cheese and basil rather than oregano, and it was stunning.

See the tips beneath the recipe for directions for making a freestyle loaf for the oven.

Ingredients

- 3 cups bread flour
- 1 cup water
- 1/2 cup newly ground cheese (Romano or Parmesan)
- 1 tablespoon dried leaf oregano
- 1/2 tablespoons olive oil
- 1 teaspoon salt
- 2 teaspoons dynamic dry yeast
- 3 tablespoons sugar

Steps to Make It

1. Add the ingredients to your bread machine adhering to the

maker's directions.

2. Set on essential or medium, and press start. I appreciate the fantastic fragrance!

3. The recipe makes one 1/2-pound loaf of bread.

4. Free Form Loaf for the Oven

5. Set up the bread in the bread machine utilizing the dough cycle.

6. Remove the dough from the machine and shape into a round loaf.

7. Spot the loaf on a material paper-fixed baking sheet and spread it with a moist kitchen towel.

8. Let it rise until multiplied, around 40 to 50 minutes.

9. Bake in a preheated 400 F oven for 25 to 30 minutes or until brilliant brown.

CHAPTER 24: BREAD MACHINE CINNAMON ROLLS

Cinnamon rolls are incredible for breakfast, nibble, and even treat. However, they can be work and time-escalated. Utilizing the bread machine slices the endeavors down the middle, depending on your bread maker to make the dough. From that point, you turn it out, sprinkle on the cinnamon-sugar filling, fold up into a log, and cut into buns. Let the cinnamon moves rise and afterward bake until puffed up and brilliant brown. Shower with the vanilla icing for that mark finish.

Ingredients

For the Dough:

- 1 cup milk
- 1 big egg
- 3 tablespoons sugar
- 1/2 teaspoon salt
- 2 teaspoons dynamic dry yeast (or 1/2 teaspoons bread machine/fast rise yeast)
- 1/4 cup (1/2 stick) spread or margarine
- 3 1/3 cups bread flour

For the Filling:

- 1/4 cup margarine (softened)
- 1/2 teaspoon nutmeg

- 1/3 cup nuts (slashed and softly toasted)
- 1/4 cup sugar
- 2 teaspoons cinnamon

For the Icing:

- 1 cup powdered sugar
- 1 to 2 tablespoons milk
- 1/2 teaspoon vanilla

Steps to Make It

Note: While there are different strides to this recipe, this cinnamon fold dish is separated into useful classes to assist you with bettering arrangements for preparation and cooking.

Make the Dough

1. Accumulate the ingredients.
2. Include the elements for the dough to your bread machine as suggested by the maker. Program the appliance for the dough cycle. Leave the dough alone kneaded and produced.
3. At the point when the cycle is done, place the dough onto a floured surface. Knead the dough for around one moment, at that point let it rest for an additional 15 minutes.
4. Make the Filling and Shape
5. Turn the dough out into a square shape, around 15 by 10 inches.
6. Brush the softened spread over the dough to inside one inch of the edges.

7. Mixture the sugar, cinnamon, nutmeg, and slashed nuts in a bowl. Sprinkle the mixture equally over dough.

8. Beginning the long side, roll the dough up firmly. Press the edges to seal and structure into a 12-inch long, equally formed roll.

9. With a blade or 8-inch-long bit of uncoated dental floss, cut the whole fold into one-inch pieces.

Rising and Baking the Dough

1. Oil a 13 by 9-inch baking dish.

2. Spot the moves chop side down in the pan. Spread and let rise in a warm, without draft place until it copies in size. This will take around 30 to 45 minutes.

3. Preheat the oven to 375 F.

4. Bake the moves for around 20 to 25 minutes or until brilliant brown.

Make the Icing and Frost

1. Assemble the ingredients.

2. Join the powdered sugar, milk, and vanilla. Mix the mixture until it is smooth. If that excessively slender or excessively thick, include progressively powdered sugar or milk, separately, until the ideal consistency is reached.

3. Cool the moves in the search for gold to 15 minutes, at that point shower them with the powdered sugar icing.

CHAPTER 25: BREAD MACHINE HOT CROSS BUNS

Hot cross buns are generally eaten on Good Friday in certain zones of America and different nations, however nowadays individuals appreciate them whenever of the year. The mark cross—speaking to the execution—is shaped on the top of every bun with icing.

These exemplary hot cross buns are begun in the bread machine, so there no manual kneading required.

The dough is mixed and kneaded in the bread machine and afterward, the rolls are formed and baked by hand. The scrumptious slight vanilla icing is showered over every bun to frame the exemplary "cross."

These are exceptionally simple to plan, thus delicate and scrumptious!

Ingredients

- 3/4 cup milk (low-fat is fine; tepid)
- 2 teaspoons vanilla concentrate
- 1 huge egg (room temperature)
- 3 cups generally useful flour
- 1/3 cup granulated sugar
- 1 teaspoon salt (inadequate)
- 3 teaspoons dynamic dry yeast
- 1/4 cup mellowed spread (slice into 4 to 6 pieces)
- 1/2 teaspoons ground cinnamon

- 3/4 to 1 cup currants (or finely hacked dried peaches)
- 1 huge egg yolk
- 2 tablespoons water

For the Icing:

- 1/2 cups powdered sugar
- 2 tablespoons milk
- 1/2 teaspoon vanilla (or vanilla bean glue)

Steps to Make It

1. Accumulate the ingredients.
2. Whisk together the 3/4 cup milk, 2 teaspoons of vanilla, and the egg.
3. Include the milk mixture, flour, granulated sugar, salt, yeast, and spread to the bread machine, including the request recommended by your bread machine maker.
4. Set the machine on the dough cycle; include cinnamon and currants or cleaved dried natural product at the signal. If that the mixture appears to be excessively dry, include water in modest quantities.
5. At the point when the dough is done and multiplied in size, evacuate to a gently floured surface. Punch down, knead around 6 to multiple times, and let it rest for 10 minutes.
6. Oil a 9-inch square baking container.
7. Remove small bits of dough (around 2 to 2 1/4 ounces each) and shape them into balls. Place the dough balls in the readied baking container. Spread the dish with a fabric and let the dough

rise in a warm spot for 40 minutes.

8. Preheat the oven to 350 F.

9. Mix the egg yolk and 2 tablespoons water. Daintily brush the tops of the buns with the egg yolk mixture. Bake for 20 to 25 minutes, until the tops are pleasantly cooked. Evacuate the pan to a rack to cool totally.

10. Consolidate the confectioners' sugar with 2 tablespoons of milk and 1/2 teaspoon vanilla; mix until smooth. Include limited quantities of high temp water or more confectioners' sugar, varying, for sprinkling consistency. With a spoon or designing pack, sprinkle crosses on the tops of the buns.

Tip

If you don't have a bread machine or if you like to knead by hand, mixture the milk and egg mixture with the flour and yeast mixture in a big bowl by hand. Move the dough to a floured surface and knead, including the currants and cinnamon in as you fold it over, until it is smooth and flexible around 10 minutes. Spread and let the dough rise until twofold, around 45 minutes. Punch it down and work 5 or multiple times. Shape the dough into balls and proceed with the recipe.

CHAPTER 26: BREAD MACHINE PUMPKIN QUICK BREAD

We made this pumpkin bread in a Zojirushi bread machine, yet it should work with any standard size bread machine with a cake or speedy bread cycle. Combine the ingredients in a bowl first to ensure they're very much consolidated.

Ingredients

- 1/3 cup vegetable oil
- 3 huge eggs
- 1/2 cups pumpkin puree (canned or homemade)
- 3/4 teaspoon ground cinnamon
- 1/4 teaspoon ground nutmeg
- 1/4 teaspoon ground ginger
- 3 cups generally useful flour
- 1/2 cup cleaved pecans or walnuts (discretionary)
- 1 cup granulated sugar
- 1/2 teaspoons baking powder
- 1/2 teaspoon baking pop
- 1/4 teaspoon salt

Steps to Make It

1. Splash bread machine pan with nonstick cooking shower or baking splash.

2. In a bowl, mixture vegetable oil, eggs, pumpkin puree, and sugar until all-around mixed.

3. Mix in the baking powder, pop, salt, flavors, and flour just until mixed.

4. Empty the hitter into the prepared bread machine pan and set on the cake or brisk bread cycle.

5. Include cleaved nuts at the signal, if utilizing.

6. Cautiously remove the loaf from the pan and paddle and turn out onto a rack to cool.

Tip

Oven Directions: In a mixing bowl, join the entirety of the ingredients, including the nuts. Bake the bread at 350 F in a lubed loaf prospect 50 to an hour, or until a toothpick embedded into the inside tells the truth.

CHAPTER 27: BREAD MACHINE BLUEBERRY ROLLS

These delicate blueberry rolls are anything but difficult to mixture and knead utilizing the bread machine, and they make an astonishing breakfast or early lunch bread. Forming the rolls is an easy task. Simply fold the dough into balls and spot them in the dish, one next to the other. They're magnificent with the icing, and one individual proposed the egg wash and a sprinkling of cinnamon-sugar.

Take a dish of these draws separated blueberry moves to the workplace or potluck.

Ingredients

- 1 cup milk (room temperature)
- 1 huge egg (room temperature)
- 2 teaspoons vanilla concentrate
- 4 tablespoons spread (mollified; in small pieces)
- 1 tablespoon dynamic dry yeast
- 3/4 to 1 cup blueberries (dried)
- 1 teaspoon cinnamon
- 1 tablespoon water
- 1 big egg yolk
- 3 1/2 cups generally useful flour
- 1/3 cup sugar
- 1 teaspoon salt

73

For the Vanilla Icing:

- 1/2 cups confectioners' sugar
- 1 tablespoon margarine (dissolved)
- 1 teaspoon vanilla concentrate
- 2 tablespoons water (hot; or milk; in addition to additional for consistency)

Steps to Make It

1. In a bowl, whisk the milk with the egg and vanilla extract.
2. To the bread machine pan in the request recommended by your machine's maker, include the milk mixture, flour, sugar, salt, spread, and yeast.
3. Start the machine on the dough cycle. Include the blueberries and ground cinnamon at the blare.
4. Oil a 9-inch round baking dish.
5. Turn the dough out onto a floured surface and punch it down. Ply a couple of times, including more flour, if necessary, to shield it from adhering to the surface and hands.
6. Shape the dough into 16 uniform balls and place them one next to the other in the readied round dish. Spread the pan with a kitchen towel and let the moves rise in a sans draft place for 40 minutes.
7. Warmth the oven to 350 F.
8. In a small bowl, whisk the water and egg yolk. Brush the mixture over the tops of the rolls.
9. Bake, the moves for 20 to 25 minutes, or until the tops, are

brilliant brown.

10. Remove the moves to a rack and let them cool for 5 to 10 minutes while you set up the icing.

Set up the Icing

1. In a bowl, join the confectioners' sugar with the dissolved margarine and 1 teaspoon of vanilla extract. Include 2 tablespoons of hot water or milk, or enough to make a decent sprinkling consistency.

2. Move the moves from the pan to a rack. Place a sheet of foil or wax paper under the rack.

3. Shower the icing over the warm rolls.

Master Tips

Cream Cheese Icing: In a bowl, consolidate 3 ounces of relaxed cream cheese with 1/2 cups of confectioners' sugar, 2 teaspoons of mollified margarine, and enough milk or creamer to make a decent consistency for sprinkling over the warm rolls.

Supplant the dried blueberries with dried cranberries or raisins.

CHAPTER 28: NURSERY VEGETABLE BREAD

Ingredients

- $1/2$ cup warm buttermilk (70° to 80°)
- 3 tablespoons water (70° to 80°)
- 1 tablespoon canola oil
- 2 tablespoons sugar
- 1 teaspoon salt
- 1/2 teaspoon lemon-pepper flavoring
- 1/2 cup antiquated oats
- 2-1/2 cups bread flour
- 1-1/2 teaspoons dynamic dry yeast
- 2/3 cup destroyed zucchini
- 1/4 cup cleaved red sweet pepper
- 2 tablespoons cleaved green onions
- 2 tablespoons ground Romano or Parmesan cheese

Instructions

1. In bread machine pan, place all ingredients all together recommended by maker. Select essential bread setting. Pick covering color and loaf size if accessible.

2. Bake as indicated by bread machine directions (check dough following 5 minutes of mixing; add 1 to 2 tablespoons of water or flour if necessary).

CHAPTER 29: ESPRESSO RAISIN BREAD

Ingredients

- 3/4 cup raisins
- 1 tablespoon in addition to 3 cups bread flour, partitioned
- 1 cup solid fermented espresso (70° to 80°)
- 3 tablespoons sugar
- 1 teaspoon ground cinnamon
- 1/4 teaspoon ground allspice
- 1/4 teaspoon ground cloves
- 2-1/2 teaspoons dynamic dry yeast
- 3 tablespoons canola oil
- 1 egg, gently beaten
- 1-1/2 teaspoons salt

Instructions

1. Hurl raisins with 1 tablespoon flour; put in a safe spot. In bread machine container, place the espresso, oil, egg, salt, sugar, flavors, yeast and remaining flour all together proposed by the maker. Select essential bread setting. Pick covering color and loaf size if accessible.
2. Bake as indicated by bread machine directions (check dough following 5 minutes of mixing; add 1 to 2 tablespoons of water or flour if necessary).

3. Not long before the last kneading (your machine may discernibly flag this), include the raisins.

CHAPTER 30: POPPY SEED LEMON BREAD

Ingredients

- 3/4 cup water ($70°$ to $80°$)
- 1 big egg
- 3 tablespoons lemon juice
- 3/4 teaspoon salt
- 3 cups bread flour
- 2 tablespoons poppy seeds
- 1/4 teaspoon ground nutmeg
- 2-1/4 teaspoons dynamic dry yeast
- 3 tablespoons spread, relaxed
- 3 tablespoons sugar
- 1 tablespoon ground lemon get-up-and-go

NUTMEG BUTTER:

- 1/2 cup spread, relaxed
- 1/2 cup confectioners' sugar
- 1/4 teaspoon ground nutmeg

Directions

1. In bread machine container, place the initial 11 ingredients all together recommended by the maker. Select essential bread setting. Pick covering color and loaf size if accessible.

79

2. Bake as per bread machine directions (check dough following 5 minutes of mixing; add 1 to 2 tablespoons of water or flour if necessary).

3. In a small bowl, consolidate nutmeg spread ingredients; beat until mixed. Refrigerate until serving.

CHAPTER 31: FOUR-HERB BREAD

Ingredients

- 1-1/4 cups water (70° to 80°)
- 2 tablespoons spread, mollified
- 3 cups bread flour
- 1 tablespoon minced new marjoram or 1 teaspoon dried marjoram
- 1 tablespoon minced new thyme or 1 teaspoon dried thyme
- 2 teaspoons minced new basil or 1/2 teaspoon dried basil
- 1 teaspoon salt
- 3 teaspoons dynamic dry yeast
- 2 tablespoons nonfat dry milk powder
- 2 tablespoons sugar
- 1 tablespoon minced chives

Directions

- In bread machine dish, place all ingredients all together recommended by the manufactures. Select fundamental bread setting. Pick covering color and loaf size if accessible. Bake as per bread machine directions (check dough following 5 minutes of mixing; add 1 to 2 tablespoons of water or flour if necessary).

81

CHAPTER 32: TURKEY STUFFING BREAD

Ingredients

- 1 cup in addition to 1 tablespoon warm milk (70° to 80°)
- 1 egg
- 1 tablespoon spread, relaxed
- 2 tablespoons brown sugar
- 1-1/2 teaspoons salt
- 1/3 cup cornmeal
- 3 cups bread flour
- 3/4 teaspoon poultry flavoring
- 1/2 teaspoon scoured sage
- 1/2 teaspoon pepper
- 2-1/4 teaspoons dynamic dry yeast
- 4-1/2 teaspoons dried minced onion
- 1-1/2 teaspoons celery seed

Headings

1. In bread machine pan, place all ingredients all together recommended by manufacturers. Select fundamental bread setting. Pick outside color and loaf size if accessible.

2. Bake as indicated by bread machine directions (check dough following 5 minutes of mixing; add 1 to 2 tablespoons of water or flour if necessary).

CHAPTER 33: FRUIT PURÉE SPICE BREAD

Ingredients

- 3/4 cup water (70° to 80°)
- 1/2 cup improved fruit purée (70° to 80°)
- 2 tablespoons brown sugar
- 3 cups bread flour
- 1/3 cup fast cooking oats
- 2 tablespoons nonfat dry milk powder
- 2-1/4 teaspoons dynamic dry yeast
- 1 tablespoon canola oil
- 1-1/2 teaspoons crusty fruit-filled treat flavor
- 3/4 teaspoon salt

Headings

1. In bread machine pan, place all ingredients all together recommended by maker. Select fundamental bread setting. Pick outside color and loaf size if accessible.

2. Check dough following 5 minutes of mixing; add 1 to 2 tablespoons of water or flour if necessary. Bake as indicated by bread machine directions.

CHAPTER 34: POPPY SEED EGG BREAD

Ingredients

- 3/4 cup water (70° to 80°)
- 1/4 cup margarine, mellowed
- 2 eggs
- 1 egg yolk
- 2 tablespoons sugar
- 1-1/2 teaspoons salt
- 1 tablespoon poppy seeds
- 3 cups bread flour
- 1-3/4 teaspoons dynamic dry yeast

Headings

In bread machine container, place all ingredients all together proposed by manufactures. Select fundamental bread setting. Pick outside layer color and loaf size if accessible. Bake as per bread machine directions (check dough following 5 minutes of mixing; add 1 to 2 tablespoons of water or flour if necessary).

CHAPTER 35: BRILLIANT ORANGE PAN ROLLS

Ingredients

- 1 can (11 ounces) mandarin oranges, depleted
- 1/2 cup Daisy 4% curds
- 2 tablespoons water
- 2 tablespoons vegetable oil
- 2 tablespoons nectar
- 1/2 teaspoon salt
- 1/2 teaspoon baking pop
- 3 cups bread flour
- 1 cup brisk cooking oats
- 2-1/2 teaspoons dynamic dry yeast
- 1 tablespoon margarine, dissolved

Instructions

1. In a bread machine pan, place the initial 10 ingredients all together recommended by the manufactures. Select dough setting. Check dough following 5 minutes of mixing (dough ought to be firm). Add 1 to 2 tablespoons of water or flour if necessary.

2. At the point when the cycle is finished, turn dough onto a delicately floured surface. Spread and let rest for 15 minutes. Roll or pat to 1/2-in. thickness. Cut with a 2-in. roll shaper.

85

Place in a lubed 13-in. x 9-in. baking pan. Brush with margarine. Spread and let rise in a warm spot until multiplied, around 60 minutes. Bake at 350° for 20-25 minutes or until brilliant brown. Serve warm.

CHAPTER 36: DELICATE ITALIAN BREADSTICKS

Ingredients

- 1 cup water (70° to 80°)
- 3 tablespoons margarine, mellowed
- 1-1/2 teaspoons salt
- 3 cups bread flour
- 2 tablespoons sugar
- 1 teaspoon Italian flavoring
- 1 teaspoon garlic powder
- 2-1/4 teaspoons dynamic dry yeast

Beating:

- 1 tablespoon margarine, liquefied
- 1 tablespoon ground Parmesan cheese

Instructions

1. In bread machine pan, place the water, margarine, salt, flour, sugar, Italian flavoring, garlic powder, and yeast all together recommended by the maker. Select dough setting (check dough following 5 minutes of mixing; add 1 to 2 tablespoons water or flour if necessary).

2. At the point when the cycle is finished, turn dough onto a gently floured surface; Divide into equal parts. Cut each segment into

12 pieces; fold each into a 4-in. to 6-in. rope. Place 2 in. separated on lubed baking sheets. Spread and let rise in a warm place until multiplied, around 20 minutes.

3. Bake at 350° for 15-18 minutes or until brilliant brown. Quickly brush with spread; sprinkle with Parmesan cheese. Serve warm.

CHAPTER 37: PEPPERONI CHEESE BREAD

Ingredients

- 1 cup water (70° to 80°)
- 1 tablespoon margarine
- 2 tablespoons sugar
- 2 teaspoons ground mustard
- 1/2 teaspoon salt
- 1/2 teaspoon cayenne pepper
- 1/4 teaspoon garlic powder
- 3 cups bread flour
- 2-1/4 teaspoons dynamic dry yeast
- 1-1/2 cups destroyed Mexican cheese mix
- 1 cup slashed pepperoni

Instructions

1. In bread machine pan, place the initial nine ingredients all together recommended by the manufactures. Select essential bread setting. Pick covering color and load size if accessible. Bake as per bread machine headings (check dough following 5 minutes of mixing; add 1 to 2 tablespoons of water or flour if necessary).
2. Not long before the last kneading (your machine may discernibly flag this), include the cheese and pepperoni.

3. Freeze alternative: Securely wrap and freeze cooled portion in foil and spot in resalable plastic cooler pack. To utilize, defrost at room temperature.

CHAPTER 38: BREAD MACHINE PUMPKIN MONKEY BREAD

Ingredients

- 1 cup warm 2% milk (70° to 80°)
- 3/4 cup canned pumpkin
- 2 tablespoons margarine, relaxed
- 1/4 cup sugar
- 1 teaspoon salt
- 1 teaspoon ground cinnamon
- 1/2 teaspoon ground ginger
- 1/4 teaspoon ground cloves
- 1/4 teaspoon ground nutmeg
- 4 to 4-1/4 cups universally handy flour
- 2 teaspoons dynamic dry yeast

SAUCE:

- 1 cup margarine, cubed
- 1 cup pressed brown sugar
- 1 cup dried cranberries
- 1/4 cup canned pumpkin
- 1 teaspoon ground cinnamon
- 1/2 teaspoon ground ginger
- 1/4 teaspoon ground nutmeg
- 1/4 teaspoon ground cloves

Instructions

1. In bread machine container, place the initial 11 ingredients all together proposed by manufactures. Select dough setting. Check dough following 5 minutes of mixing; include 1-2 tablespoons of water or flour if necessary.

2. In the meantime, in a huge pot, consolidate sauce ingredients; cook and mix until mixed. Remove from bake.

3. At the point when the dough cycle is finished, turn dough onto a delicately floured surface. Separation into 36 parts; shape into balls.

4. Organize half of the balls in a lubed 10-in. fluted tube pan; spread with half of the sauce. Repeat, being certain to completely cover the top layer with sauce.

5. Give rise access a warm place until multiplied, around 30 minutes. Preheat oven to 375°. Bake 20-25 minutes or until brilliant brown. Spread freely with foil if top browns too rapidly.

6. Cool in pan 10 minutes before altering onto a serving plate. Serve warm.

CHAPTER 39: FRIDGE BUTTERHORNS

Ingredients

- 2 bundles (1/4 ounce every) dynamic dry yeast
- 1/4 cup warm water (110° to 115°)
- 2 cups warm 2%milk (110° to 115°)
- 3/4 cup margarine, liquefied
- 1/2 cup sugar
- 1 big egg, room temperature
- 1 teaspoon salt
- 6-1/2 cups universally handy flour
- Extra liquefied margarine

Headings

1. In a small bowl, break down yeast in warm water. In a big bowl, consolidate the milk, spread, sugar, egg, salt, yeast mixture, and 3 cups flour; beat on medium speed until smooth. Mix in enough outstanding flour to frame a delicate dough (dough will be sticky).

2. Try not to ply. Spot in a lubed bowl, going once to oil the top. Cover and refrigerate for the time being.

3. Punch down dough. Turn onto a softly floured surface; Divide down the middle. Fold each into a 12-in. circle; cut each into 12 wedges. Move up wedges from the wide finishes. Place 2 in.

separated on lubed baking sheets, point side down. Spread with kitchen towels; let rise in a warm place until multiplied, around 60 minutes.

4. Bake at 350° for 15-20 minutes or until brilliant brown. Quickly brush with extra dissolved spread. Remove from container to wire racks to cool.

CHAPTER 40: APPLE BREAD

Ingredients

- 3 cups generally useful flour
- 2 cups sugar
- 2 teaspoons ground cinnamon
- 1 teaspoon baking pop
- 1/2 teaspoon baking powder
- 1/2 teaspoon salt
- 4 huge eggs, room temperature
- 1 cup canola oil
- 1/2 teaspoon vanilla concentrate
- 2 cups hacked stripped apples (around 2 medium)
- 1 cup of hacked pecans

Directions

1. Preheat oven to 350° Line 2 lubed 8x4-in. loaf container with material; oil material.
2. Whisk together initial 6 ingredients. In another bowl, whisk together eggs, oil, and vanilla; add to flour mixture, mixing just until saturated (hitter will be thick). Overlay in apples and pecans.
3. Move to an arranged dish. Bake until a toothpick embedded in focus tells the truth, 50-55 minutes. Cool in dish 10 minutes before removing to wire racks to cool.
4. Freeze choice: Securely wrap cooled loaves in plastic and foil,

at that point freeze. To utilize, defrost at room temperature.

CHAPTER 41: FESTIVITY BRAID

Ingredients

- 2 bundles (1/4 ounce every) dynamic dry yeast
- 1 cup warm water (110° to 115°)
- 2 huge eggs
- 1/3 cup spread, mellowed
- 1/4 cup sugar
- 1 teaspoon salt
- 4-1/2 to 5 cups generally useful flour
- 1 huge egg yolk
- 1 tablespoon water

Directions

1. In a small bowl, break down yeast in warm water. In a big bowl, join eggs, spread, sugar, salt, yeast mixture, and 3 cups flour; beat on medium speed 3 minutes. Mix in enough outstanding flour to frame delicate dough.

2. On a floured surface, knead dough until smooth and versatile, 6-8 minutes. Spot in a lubed bowl, going once to oil the top. Spread and let rise in a warm spot until multiplied, around 60 minutes.

3. Punch down dough. Turn onto a softly floured surface; Divide into four segments. Shape each into an 18-in. rope. Spot ropes one next to the other on a lubed baking sheet. Starting toward one side, interlace dough by setting the primary rope throughout

97

the subsequent rope, under the third and over the fourth. Repeat three or multiple times, starting each time from a similar end. Squeeze closures to seal; fold under.

4. Spread with a kitchen towel; let rise in a warm spot until multiplied, around 45 minutes. Preheat oven to 350°.

5. Whisk egg yolk with water; brush over twist. Bake until brilliant brown, 20-25 minutes. Remove from pan to a wire rack to cool.

CHAPTER 42: DATE PECAN TEA BREAD

Ingredients

- 2-1/2 cups cleaved dates
- 1-1/2 cups bubbling water
- 1-1/2 teaspoons baking pop
- 1-3/4 cups generally useful flour
- 1/4 teaspoon each ground cloves, cinnamon, ginger and nutmeg
- 2 tablespoons margarine, mellowed
- 1-1/4 cups sugar
- 1 big egg
- 2 teaspoons vanilla concentrate

SPREAD:

- 3 ounces cream cheese, mellowed
- 2 tablespoons cleaved dates
- 2 tablespoons paddle cleaved walnuts
- 1 tablespoon 2% milk

Instructions

1. Place dates in an big bowl. Join bubbling water and baking pop; pour over dates. In a small bowl, consolidate the flour, cloves, cinnamon, ginger and nutmeg; put in a safe spot.
2. In another big bowl, beat margarine and sugar until brittle. Beat

in egg and vanilla. Include flour mixture on the other hand with date mixture. Mix in walnuts.

3. Fill a lubed and floured 9x5-in. loaf container. Bake at 350° for 65-75 minutes or until a toothpick embedded in the middle confesses all. Cool for 10 minutes before removing from container to wire rack to cool totally.

4. In a small bowl, join spread ingredients. Cover and refrigerate for 60 minutes. Present with bread.

CHAPTER 43: CINNAMON SWIRL BREAD

Ingredients

- 2 bundles (1/4 ounce every) dynamic dry yeast
- 1/3 cup warm water ($110°$ to $115°$)
- 1 cup warm entire milk ($110°$ to $115°$)
- 1 cup sugar, isolated
- 2 big eggs, room temperature
- 6 tablespoons margarine, mollified
- 1-1/2 teaspoons salt
- 5-1/2 to 6 cups universally handy flour
- 2 tablespoons ground cinnamon

Instructions

1. In a big bowl, break down yeast in warm water. Include milk, 1/2 cup sugar, eggs, spread, salt, and 3 cups flour; beat on medium speed until smooth. Mix in enough outstanding flour to shape delicate dough.

2. Turn dough onto a floured surface; work until smooth and flexible, 6-8 minutes. Spot in a lubed bowl, going once to oil the top. Spread; let rise in a warm place until multiplied, around 60 minutes.

3. Mixture cinnamon and remaining sugar. Punch down dough. Turn onto a delicately floured surface; divide down the middle.

Fold each segment into 18x8-in. square shape; sprinkle each with around 1/4 cup cinnamon sugar to inside 1/2 in. of edges. Move up jam move style, beginning with a short side; squeeze fold to seal. Spot in 2 lubed 9x5-in. loaf dish, fold side down.

4. Spread with kitchen towels; let rise in a warm spot until multiplied, around 1-1/2 hours. Preheat oven to 350°.

5. Bake until brilliant brown, 30-35 minutes. Remove from container to wire racks to cool.

CHAPTER 44: WILD RICE BREAD WITH SUNFLOWER SEEDS

Ingredients

- 2 bundles (1/4 ounce every) dynamic dry yeast
- 1 cup warm water (110° to 115°)
- 1 bundle (8.8 ounces) baked to-serve long grain and wild rice
- 1 cup in addition to 1 tablespoon unsalted sunflower parts, partitioned
- 1 cup warm sans fat milk (110° to 115°)
- 1/3 cup nectar or molasses
- 1/4 cup margarine, mellowed
- 2 tablespoons ground flaxseed
- 2 teaspoons salt
- 3 cups entire wheat flour
- 2-3/4 to 3-1/4 cups universally handy flour
- 1 big egg white, gently beaten
- 1 tablespoon toasted wheat germ, discretionary

Instructions

1. In a small bowl, disintegrate yeast in warm water. In a big bowl, join rice, 1 cup sunflower bits, milk, nectar, spread, flaxseed, salt, yeast mixture, entire wheat flour, and 1 cup generally useful flour; beat on medium speed until consolidated. Mix in enough residual flour to shape a solid dough (dough will be

103

sticky).

2. Turn dough onto a floured surface; ply until versatile, around 6-8 minutes. Place in a lubed bowl, going once to oil the top. Spread with plastic wrap and let rise in a warm place until multiplied, around 1-1/4 hours.

3. Punch down dough. Turn onto a softly floured surface; separate fifty-fifty. Fold every half into a 12x8-in. square shape. Move up jam move style, beginning with a short side; squeeze fold and finishes to seal. Place each in a 9x5-in. loaf container covered with cooking shower, fold side down.

4. Spread with kitchen towels; let rise in a warm spot until nearly multiplied, around 45 minutes. Preheat oven to 375°.

5. Brush loaves with egg white; sprinkle with residual sunflower parts and, whenever wanted, wheat germ. Bake 35-45 minutes or until dim brilliant brown. Cool in pan 5 minutes. Remove to a wire rack to cool.

CONCLUSION

While utilizing a bread machine for some may seem like n unnecessary step,, others don't envision life without newly home-baked bread.

You can enjoy the newly baked handmade bread. Most bread producers likewise feature a timer function, which permits you to set the bake cycle at a specific time. This is helpful when you need to have hot bread for breakfast.

You can control what you eat. By baking bread at home, you can control what portion is coming into your loaf – this is extremely helpful for individuals with allergies or for those, who attempt to control the consumption of some of the ingredients.

A bread machine is quite easy. Some people think baking bread at home is untidy and generally, it is a hard procedure. However, baking bread with a bread machine is simple. You simply pick the ideal alternative and unwind - all the blending, rising, and heating/baking process is going on within the bread maker, which likewise makes it a zero mess process!

It saves you a lot of money in the long haul. If you feel that purchasing bread at a store is inexpensive, you may be mistaken. In turns out that in the long haul, making bread at home will save you cash, particularly if you have some dietary limitations.

Bread machines can create different sorts of bread: sans gluten bread, whole wheat bread, rye bread, and many other sports. They can also make pasta dough, pizza dough, jam, and various tasty dishes.

Extraordinary taste and quality. You have to acknowledge it – nothing beats the quality and taste of a fresh heap of bread. Since you are the one making bread, you can ensure that you utilize just the fixings that are new and of a high caliber. Homemade bread consistently beats locally acquired bread in terms of quality and taste.

Made in the USA
Monee, IL
14 May 2020

31056860R00059